International Food Library

FOOD IN GERMANY

International Food Library

FOOD IN
GERMANY

text by
Nancy Loewen

recipes compiled by
Judith A. Ahlstrom

Rourke Publications, Inc.
Vero Beach, Florida 32964

Library of Congress Cataloging-in-Publication Data

Loewen, Nancy, 1964-
   Food in Germany / by Nancy Loewen
     p. cm. — (International food library)
   Includes index.
   Summary: Describes the food products, cooking and eating customs, and festivals of Germany.
   ISBN 0-86625-347-5
   1. Cookery, German—Juvenile literature.   2. Germany—Social life and customs—Juvenile literature.   [1. Cookery, German. 2. Germany—Social life and customs.]   I. Title.   II. Series.
TX721.L58   1991
641.5943—dc20   90-21270
                                               CIP

PRINTED IN THE USA   AC

CONTENTS

A CHANGING NATION

For 28 years, the Berlin Wall marked the boundary between East and West Berlin. Made of concrete slabs, topped by barbed wire, and patrolled by armed guards, the Berlin Wall was a stark reminder of a divided Germany.

Dramatic events in the fall of 1989 changed all that. Pressured by its people, the Communist government in East Germany collapsed. For the first time since World War II, East Berliners were allowed to move freely between the two parts of the city. Instead of fearing the Wall, people gathered around it by the thousands and began to tear it down. Together, they danced, cried, and drank toasts to their new-found freedom.

This picture, taken in East Berlin in 1961, shows some of the destructive effects of World War II.

The borders and government of present-day Germany have changed many times throughout history. In fact, Germany wasn't united as one nation until 1871, when Otto von Bismarck, Prime Minister of Prussia, helped found the German Empire. Germany remained an empire until 1918, when it was defeated in World War I. At that time, pressured by the Allied powers (and also by the German people themselves), Germany was declared a republic.

The years following World War I were troubled ones for the German people. The economy was in a shambles, and the political situation was very unstable. Then a world-wide depression hit in the 1930's, and things got even worse. It was at this point that Adolph Hitler rose to power. This dictator formed the National Socialist German Worker's Party—the Nazis.

On September 1, 1939, Hitler invaded Poland, and World War II began. For several years Hitler seemed unstoppable. Beginning in 1942, however, the Allied powers began to drive the Germans back. On April 30, 1945, Adolph Hitler committed suicide in Berlin just as Soviet forces overtook the city. The Germans surrendered eight days later.

THE TWO GERMANYS

After World War II, Germany was occupied by four Allied powers—Great Britain, France, the United States, and the Soviet Union. These countries couldn't agree on how to rebuild Germany's shattered political and economic system. As a result of this disagreement, Germany was eventually divided into two nations.

West Germany, or the Federal Republic of Germany, consisted of the land that had been occupied by the British, French, and Americans. East Germany, or the German Democratic Republic, consisted of the land that had been occupied by the Soviet Union. The city of Berlin itself—Germany's pre-war capital—was split into East and West Berlin. East Berlin remained the capital of East Germany, while West Germany established Bonn as its capital.

In this 1961 photo, a resident of East Berlin points out Hitler's last headquarters, which were underground.

The Reichstag, or German Parliament building, was built in Berlin in the late 1800's. It survived a fire in 1933 and Allied bombs at the end of World War II.

The two countries were very different politically. West Germany was a democracy, while in East Germany all political power was held by the Communist Party. The border between the two countries was heavily guarded—East Germans were not allowed to travel freely, and many families and friends were separated. The Berlin Wall was put up in 1961 by the East German government to prevent its people from escaping to the West.

Today, the Berlin Wall is gone, and Germany is a unified nation once again. On October 3, 1990, the two countries were formally united in a ceremony at the Reichstag building in Berlin. The first joint election was held on December 2, 1990. Helmut Kohl, formerly the Chancellor of West Germany, was elected to lead the reunified nation.

INSIDE GERMANY

Located in central Europe, Germany occupies an area of nearly 138,000 square miles, and has a population of nearly 78 million. Berlin is once again the capital of Germany. Other major cities include Bonn, Hamburg, Munich, Cologne, Essen, Frankfurt, Leipzig, and Dresden.

Germany is made up of several distinct land regions. Northern Germany consists of low, flat plains. Central Germany is an area of plateaus broken by hilly areas. Southern Germany is an area of hills and mountains, with rich farmland in the valleys. Along the southern border of Germany stand the snow-capped Bavarian Alps. These mountains are part of a large mountain range that extends across southern Europe. Many small German villages are found here, as well as many famous winter resorts.

Legend surrounds Watzmann Mountain, part of the Bavarian Alps. According to the story, the mountain was once an evil king whom God punished by turning into stone!

Because the land in northern Germany is quite flat, the rivers there flow gently.

In the southwest corner of Germany is the famous Black Forest. This mountainous area is covered with fir and spruce trees. It provides the setting for many German fairy tales. Long ago, the Black Forest was surrounded by myth—people believed that the forest was full of wild beasts, and that a person was sure to get lost among the dense trees. Today, however, roads, railroads, and even walking trails have been built throughout the region.

Most of Germany's weather is rather mild, due to its location near the sea. Summers don't get very hot, and winters aren't very cold. Rain falls throughout much of the year. Farther inland and in mountainous areas, however, there is more contrast between the seasons.

11

GERMANY'S AGRICULTURE & INDUSTRY

At the end of World War II, the German economy was virtually shut down. Factories were in ruins. Railroad tracks and roads were destroyed. Fuel and water were in short supply.

During the 1950's and 1960's, however, both East and West Germany made a remarkable economic recovery. This turn-around was due mainly to an emphasis on manufacturing. Before long, West Germany had one of the world's highest standards of living. East Germany's standard of living became the best of any of the communist nations of Eastern Europe.

Manufacturing is still very important in Germany. Steel, automobiles, machinery, ships, chemicals, textiles, electrical equipment, and cameras are among the products Germany manufactures today.

Germany is famous for the large equipment it manufactures.

German farmers raise a lot of livestock. These cattle are grazing in southern Germany near Munich.

The Ruhr is Germany's main industrial area. It is located in west-central Germany, between the Ruhr and Lippe Rivers. More than eight million people live and work in this area, making the Ruhr one of the biggest industrial regions in the world.

Agriculture, too, has made progress since World War II. However, Germany must still import about a third of its food in order to feed its large population. German farmers raise cattle, pigs, and sheep. They cultivate many different crops, including potatoes, sugar beets, and grains. Vegetables, apples, and grapes are also grown in large quantities.

Germany's most famous beverage, beer, is produced all over the country and sold around the world. Wine, too is an important product. Germany's vineyards are located farther north than those in any other wine-producing country. The weather of any given year has a big effect on the quality of the wines.

HOLIDAYS IN GERMANY

While the German people have a reputation for being hard workers, they also have a reputation for enjoying themselves. Each fall, the city of Munich holds a celebration called *Oktoberfest*—it's sometimes called "the largest festival in the world." Oktoberfest begins in mid-September and runs through early October. During that time, the streets of Munich are transformed into a colorful maze of beer tents, parades, fairs, dancing, and exhibitions. Nearly six million visitors take part in the festivities—Germans as well as foreigners. Oktoberfest has been celebrated for nearly two centuries. The holiday dates back to a large celebration in 1810, when King Ludwig I of Bavaria married the Princess of Saxony.

Revelers fill the streets of Munich during Oktoberfest.

Neuschwanstein is only one of several castles built by King Ludwig II.

Fasching, or the carnival season, goes back to ancient times. Trying to scare the forces of winter away, the early Germans wore frightening masks. They played drums, rattles, and cymbals in haunting rhythms. Today, in the weeks before Lent, masked balls and parades are held in towns and cities all across Germany.

Christmas in Germany is a more private holiday, celebrated with family and friends. The Germans were the first people to decorate Christmas trees—a tradition that is now practiced throughout the world. Many special foods are made, such as butter cookies, Christmas breads with nuts and candied fruits, and gingerbread. On Christmas Eve, some families serve carp as a traditional meal. The fish isn't scaled, so that at the meal, everyone can get one scale for good luck in the coming year. Also, before the carp is cooked, it is scalded with boiling vinegar. This makes the carp very shimmery and attractive on the platter.

During the spring and summer, just about every town and city holds a festival of some sort. Some festivals celebrate German cultural life, such as opera, ballet, music of all kinds, and theater. Others may be more sports-oriented, revolving around events such as horse races, boating, or shooting contests.

FOOD CUSTOMS IN GERMANY

Germany is famous for its good, hearty food—and for the large quantities in which the food is served! German cooking, however, does vary quite a bit. Dishes found in one region might not be found outside that area. In general, people in northern Germany eat more vegetables and potatoes, while people in the southern regions eat more pasta and soups. Even so, there are some features of German cooking that are common throughout the country.

Pork is the most popular meat among Germans. Veal, too, is served frequently. Many kinds of sausages are made in Germany—the most famous one being the frankfurter, which originated in the city of Frankfurt. Germany also has many varieties of cheese, such as Münster and Limburger.

Fresh fruits and vegetables make a colorful display at a market in Bonn.

Cabbage fields can be found throughout the countryside in Germany.

The most common vegetables in Germany include beets, onions, carrots, turnips, and cabbage. *Sauerkraut* is a very old German dish, and can be served plain or as an ingredient in other dishes. It is made by fermenting finely cut cabbage in its own juice. Starchy foods, such as potatoes, bread, and dumplings, also play a big part in German cuisine. There are hundreds of kinds of bread, rolls, cakes, and pastries to choose from!

Breakfast in Germany is usually a small meal, consisting of fresh rolls, jam or honey, and coffee. Most Germans eat breakfast quite early—around 7 o'clock. By midmorning, it's time for *Brotzeit*, or a second breakfast. Rolls, sausage, and cheese may be offered at this time, along with mineral water, apple juice, or perhaps beer. Lunch is served at midday, and is the biggest meal of the day. In the afternoon, many Germans stop at cafés for a snack of coffee and pastries. Supper is generally a rather light meal.

17

REGIONAL COOKING IN GERMANY

Germany is bordered by the North Sea to the northwest, and the Baltic Sea to the northeast. It's not surprising, then, that cooks in the northern part of Germany make use of seafood—particularly eel, lobster, and herring. Herbed eel soup is a specialty in the cities of Hamburg and Bremen. So is *Labskaus*, which is made from herring, pickled pork, and potatoes, topped with fried eggs. Labskaus is traditionally eaten at ship launchings.

Meats and sausages are featured in central Germany. Westphalian hams are famous throughout Germany, and can weigh more than 30 pounds. The ham is often served with a specially baked pumpernickel bread. Lamb dishes are common in the Lower Saxony region, where sheep graze on the rolling hills.

Fresh fish and seafood are staple foods in northern Germany.

Surrounded by food, a Bavarian chef toasts his good fortune.

Sauerbraten is the best-known specialty of the Rhineland, the area in western Germany along the Rhine River. To make this dish, beef is marinated in vinegar and spices for several days, then simmered in red wine. Sauerbraten may be served with red cabbage, Brussel sprouts, or stewed apples.

In Swabia, the south-central region of Germany, *Spätzle* accompany roasts and other dishes. Spätzle are tiny homemade noodles, made from flour, eggs, and salt. Pancakes called *Pfannkuchen* are another common dish. The pancakes may be filled with meat, cheese, or jam. They might also be cut into strips and put into a clear soup, called *Fläddlesuppe*.

In Bavaria, a region in southern Germany, dumplings are included in many dishes. The dumplings may be made from either potatoes or bread. Some dumplings contain meats, such as liver or bacon.

A FESTIVE MEAL

Creamed Herring
German Potato Soup
Cucumber and Sour Cream Salad
Rolladen
Your choice of potato and vegetable
Baked Apples

Rolladen is one of Germany's best-known beef dishes. It takes some time to prepare, but remember—preparation is half the fun of cooking! The courses in this festive German meal should be served separately, allowing plenty of time for conversation between each one. Germans might finish this meal with a selection of fresh fruit and cheese.

German Potato Soup

2 large raw potatoes
6 stalks celery
1 pound tomatoes, peeled
2 carrots
2 leeks
1/2 pound green beans
1 pound round steak or other beefsteak, cubed
salt and pepper to taste
1 teaspoon paprika
1/4 cup parsley, chopped
1/4 cup chives, chopped
4 beef bouillon cubes

1. Wash the vegetables and cut into bite-size pieces.
2. Put the vegetables, meat, salt, paprika, herbs, and beef bouillon in a large pot and fill with water. Bring to a boil, reduce heat, and simmer for 3 hours. Serves 6–8.

Creamed Herring

1 16–20 ounce jar herring cutlets
8 ounces sour cream
$1/4$ cup milk
1 cucumber, sliced
1 firm apple, chopped
2 small onions, finely chopped
2 tablespoons chives, finely chopped

1. Drain the herring cutlets and put them in a serving dish. Add cucumber, apple, and onion.
2. Stir sour cream and milk together, then pour into the dish. Mix all ingredients until well coated with sour cream. Garnish with chives. Serves 6–8.

Cucumber and Sour Cream Salad

Cucumber and Sour Cream Salad

4 cucumbers, peeled and sliced thinly
salt and pepper to taste
$1/4$ cup fresh dill, chopped
2 tablespoons wine vinegar
8 ounces sour cream
$1/4$ cup milk

1. In a serving dish, beat the sour cream and milk with a fork until smooth. Stir in the cucumbers, salt and pepper, dill, and vinegar. Chill one hour and serve. Serves 6–8.

Rolladen

6 pieces beef round steak, about ¼ inch thick and
    4 x 10 inches in size
salt and pepper to taste
6 heaping teaspoons of mustard
2 cups onion, finely chopped
6 strips bacon
6 dill pickle spears
4 tablespoons butter
1 tablespoon paprika
1 10 ½ -ounce can beef broth
2 tablespoons corn starch (or flour)
½ cup water

1. Put the beef strips on a cutting board. Spread each with 1 heaping teaspoon of mustard and sprinkle with salt, pepper, and 4 tablespoons chopped onion.
2. Cut each bacon strip in half, then cut each half lengthwise. Arrange 4 pieces horizontally on beef.
3. Split each dill spear in half lengthwise and put 2 pieces on each beef strip in between bacon strips.
4. Roll the beef strip up and tie with string. 2 pieces of string work best, tying close to each end.
5. Heat the butter in a large frying pan. Add paprika and remaining onion and cook until onion is clear and soft. Then fry the beef rolls in the pan, turning frequently until browned.
6. Add ½ can beef broth, cover, and cook on medium heat about 45 minutes. Turn the meat, add the other ½ can of beef broth, and cook 45 minutes longer, or until tender. Remove the meat to serving platter.
7. Mix cornstarch and water. Whisk the mixture into the hot pan juices until it thickens. Pour gravy over meat on platter. Serves 6–8.

Rolladen

Baked Apples

> 1 package frozen puff pastry
> 6 apples
> 6 tablespoons sliced almonds
> 6 tablespoons raisins
> $1/3$ cup sugar
> 6 teaspoons red currant jelly
> 1 egg, beaten

1. Roll the dough out thinly. Cut into squares large enough to cover one apple. Wash, peel, and take the core out of the apples. Mix the almonds, raisins, sugar, and jelly in a bowl.
2. Place an apple on a square of pastry dough. Fill the center with the almond mixture. Moisten the edges of the pastry with water, using your finger. Pull the edges together at the top of the apple and press together firmly.
3. Prick the dough all over with a fork. Brush with the beaten egg. Bake in a greased cake pan about 45 minutes at 350°. When the crust begins to sag, the apple should be done cooking. Cool about 15 minutes and serve with vanilla ice cream. Serves 6.

A MEAL FROM THE RHINELAND

Sauerbraten with Noodles
Your choice of vegetable
Berlin Cream Pancakes

Sauerbraten

3 pounds beef round steak
1/4 cup whole peppercorns
1 tablespoon mustard seeds
1 tablespoon whole cloves
2 bay leaves
3 onions, chopped
2 cups white vinegar
1/4 cup butter
2 10 1/2 -ounce cans beef broth
2 tablespoons flour
1/4 cup water
2 tablespoons whipping cream

1. Trim excess fat from meat. Cut meat into 8 pieces and place in a large glass cake pan. Mix the peppercorns, mustard seed, cloves, bay leaves, onion, and vinegar and pour over meat. Cover and put in the refrigerator for 3 days. Turn meat occasionally.
2. Drain off the marinade into a measuring cup. Add 1/4 cup butter and 1/2 of the marinade to the meat. Bake at 350° for 1 hour.
3. Turn the meat over and place strips of bacon over the meat. Cook 1 more hour or until meat is tender. Turn the oven to 200°. Place the meat on a platter and return to oven to keep warm.
4. Strain the marinade into a large pan. Add the beef broth and bring to a boil. Mix the flour and water in a jar, shaking to blend. Remove liquid from heat, add flour, and stir. Return to heat, stirring until it boils again. Cook about 5 minutes on medium-low heat, stirring frequently.
5. Just before serving, remove gravy from heat, stir in cream and pour over meat. Serve with noodles. Serves 6.

**Berlin Pancakes
are rich and filling,
so be sure to save
plenty of room!**

Berlin Cream Pancakes

1 cup flour
4 eggs (separate yolks and whites)
²/₃ cup sour cream
¹/₃ cup milk
¹/₂ teaspoon salt
1 tablespoon sugar
butter or margarine
¹/₄ teaspoon ground cinnamon
4 tablespoons jam
1 cup whipping cream
2 tablespoons sugar
¹/₂ teaspoon vanilla extract

1. Whisk flour, egg yolks, sour cream, milk, salt, and 1 tablespoon sugar until batter is smooth.
2. Beat egg whites until they're very stiff, then stir them into the batter.
3. Cook 6 pancakes in a frying pan that is greased with butter or margarine. Use about ¹/₂ cup of batter for each pancake.
4. Beat whipping cream until it is stiff. Stir in vanilla and 2 tablespoons sugar.
5. Spoon jam and whipped cream on top of pancakes. Sprinkle with cinnamon. Serves 6.

A MEAL FROM BAVARIA

Bavarian Pork Roast
Potato Dumplings
Hunter's Cabbage

No Bavarian meal would be complete without dumplings. The trick to tasty dumplings is to cook them just the right amount of time.

Bavarian Pork Roast

    3 ¹/₂ pounds boneless pork shoulder roast
    pepper to taste
    5 tablespoons butter
    2 ¹/₂ cups onion, chopped
    8 cloves garlic, peeled and sliced
    2 tablespoons caraway seeds
    1 tablespoon marjoram
    1 cup water

1. Preheat oven to 350°. Cut the roast in 6–8 slices. Sprinkle both sides with pepper.
2. In a large roasting pan, melt the butter on top of the stove. Put the meat in pan and cover with onion, garlic, caraway seeds, and marjoram. Add the water and bake for 2 hours. Do not cover.
3. Turn the meat over, add more water if necessary and bake for 1 more hour. Serves 6–8.

Potato Dumplings

    6 medium white potatoes
    2 eggs
    2 teaspoons salt
    ²/₃ cup flour
    ²/₃ cup butter
    ¹/₃ cup bread crumbs

1. Boil the potatoes with the skins on, until soft (about 30 minutes). Do not cover the pan. Cool, then peel.
2. Mash potatoes using an electric beater. Add eggs, salt, and flour. Whip again until fluffy.

Potato Dumplings

3. Wet your hands with water. Roll mixture into 1-inch balls. Drop into boiling, salted water and cook 10–15 minutes on medium heat. Remove with slotted spoon and drain water. Place in serving dish.
4. Melt the butter, stir in bread crumbs, and pour over dumplings just before serving. Serves 6–8.

Hunter's Cabbage

6 slices bacon
1 cup onion, chopped
3 tablespoons white wine
2 soft apples, peeled and sliced
1 small head white cabbage, chopped
1 tablespoon flour
1 10 ½-ounce can beef broth
salt and pepper to taste
2 beef bouillon cubes

1. Cook the bacon. Drain on paper towels and break into pieces. Cook onion in bacon fat until soft. Add white wine, apple slices, and bouillon cubes.
2. Add cabbage and simmer with the other ingredients for 30 minutes, stirring frequently.
3. Sprinkle flour over cabbage, pour in broth, and stir until a creamy white sauce forms. Season with salt and pepper.

AN EVERYDAY MEAL

Roasted Sauerkraut
and Pork
Boiled Potatoes

Even people who
hate sauerkraut will
love this dish!

2 pounds boneless pork shoulder roast
2–3 tablespoons cooking oil
2 cups onion, chopped
1 bay leaf
1 tablespoon paprika
2 cups tomatoes, chopped
2 16-ounce cans sauerkraut, drained thoroughly
1 cup onion, chopped
10 peppercorns
1 10 $^1/_2$ -ounce can chicken broth
1 cup white wine
1 teaspoon caraway seeds
$^1/_2$ teaspoon garlic, chopped

1. Cut the roast into 2-inch chunks. Sprinkle meat
   with salt and pepper.
2. Heat oil in large oven-proof pan on top of stove.
   Brown meat well. Bake at 350°, uncovered, about 15
   minutes.
3. Remove from oven and add onions, bay leaf, and
   paprika. Cook on stove until onion is soft. Add
   tomatoes. Bake 1½ hours at 300°.
4. Put sauerkraut, onion, garlic, caraway seeds,
   peppercorns, wine, and broth into a large pot. Bring
   to a boil; reduce heat, cover, and simmer for 1 hour.
5. Combine pork with sauerkraut in a large bowl.
   Serve with boiled potatoes. Serves 4–6.

GLOSSARY OF COOKING TERMS

For those readers who are less experienced in the kitchen, the following list explains the cooking terms used in this book.

Chopped	Cut into small pieces measuring about ½ inch thick. Finely chopped pieces should be about ⅛ inch thick.
Diced	Cut into small cubes.
Garnished	Decorated.
Grated	Cut into small pieces by using a grater.
Greased	Having been lightly coated with oil, butter, or margarine to prevent sticking.
Knead	To work dough with one's hands.
Marinate	To cover and soak with a mixture of juices, called a marinade.
Minced	Chopped into very tiny pieces.
Pinch	The amount you can pick up between your thumb and forefinger.
Reserve	To set aside an ingredient for future use.
Sauté	To cook food in oil, butter, or margarine at high temperature, while stirring constantly.
Shredded	Cut into lengths of 1–2 inches, about ¼ inch across. Finely shredded ingredients should be about ⅛ inch across.
Simmer	To cook on a stove at the lowest setting.
Sliced	Cut into thin slices that show the original shape of the object.
Toss	To mix the ingredients in a salad.
Whisk	To beat using a hand whisk or electric mixer.

GERMAN COOKING

To make the recipes in this book, you will need the following equipment and ingredients, which may not be in your kitchen:

Beef bouillon cubes Can be found in the soup section of supermarkets.

Bread crumbs Prepared bread crumbs can be bought at a supermarket. You can make your own by crushing dried bread with a rolling pin.

Crayfish tails Fresh crayfish can now be found in many supermarkets. Shrimp is a good substitute and is available in almost any supermarket.

Garlic Fresh garlic can be bought in supermarkets. Each bulb can be broken into sections called cloves. You have to remove the brittle skin around each clove before chopping it.

Herbs Fresh bay leaves, chives, and dill can be found in the produce section of many supermarkets. Dried versions can be found in the spice section.

Herring cutlets Can be found in the meat section of almost any supermarket.

Leeks These onions are available in the produce section of most supermarkets.

Morel mushrooms These wild mushrooms are available in some supermarkets only in the early summer. You can substitute regular mushrooms.

Puff pastry This item is found in the frozen food section of supermarkets.

Spices Caraway seeds, cloves, mustard seeds, nutmeg, paprika, peppercorns, and vanilla extract are found in the spice section of supermarkets.

A waitress serves large steins of German beer.

INDEX

We would like to thank and acknowledge the following people for the use of their photographs and transparencies:

Mark E. Ahlstrom: cover, 7, 8, 13, 15, 17, 21, 23, 25, 27, 28; German Information Center: cover inset, 2, 9, 10, 11, 12, 14, 16, 18, 19, 30.

Produced by Mark E. Ahlstrom (The Bookworks)
Typesetting and layout by The Final Word
Photo research by Judith Ahlstrom